BLACK HISTORY

Slavery

By James De Medeiros

www.av2books.com

AV² provides enriched content that supplements and complements this book. Weigl's AV² books strive to create inspired learning and engage young minds in a total learning experience.

Your AV² Media Enhanced books come alive with...

Audio
Listen to sections of the book read aloud.

Key Words
Study vocabulary, and complete a matching word activity.

Video
Watch informative video clips.

Quizzes
Test your knowledge.

Embedded Weblinks
Gain additional information for research.

Slide Show
View images and captions, and prepare a presentation.

Try This!
Complete activities and hands-on experiments.

... and much, much more!

Go to **www.av2books.com**, and enter this book's unique code.

BOOK CODE

E159101

AV² by Weigl brings you media enhanced books that support active learning.

Download the AV² catalog at **www.av2books.com/catalog**

AV² Online Navigation on page 48

Published by AV² by Weigl
350 5th Avenue, 59th Floor
New York, NY 10118
Website: www.av2books.com   www.weigl.com

Library of Congress Cataloging-in-Publication Data

De Medeiros, James, 1975–
  Slavery / James de Medeiros.
    p. cm. -- (Black history)
  Includes index.
  ISBN 978-1-62127-195-6 (hardcover : alk. paper) -- ISBN 978-1-62127-201-4 (softcover : alk. paper)
  1. Slavery--United States--History--Juvenile literature. 2. Slave insurrections--United States--History--Juvenile literature. 3. African Americans--History--To 1863--Juvenile literature. I. Title.
  E441.D342 2013
  306.3'620973--dc23
                    2012040623

Printed in the United States of America in North Mankato, Minnesota
1 2 3 4 5 6 7 8 9 0 17 16 15 14 13 12

112012
WEP301112

Weigl acknowledges Getty Images as its primary image supplier for this title.

Editor: Heather Kissock
Designer: Terry Paulhus

Contents

Africans Enslaved

On July 4, 1776, the United States declared its independence from Great Britain. It became a free country on that day, but still kept many of the traditions and ideas of Great Britain, including slavery.

British colonists were the first to bring Africans to the United States. Millions of people were kidnapped in Africa and brought to the United States on boats. They were considered the property of the people who owned them and were forced to work in poor conditions. Many were whipped and beaten by their **masters**.

Abolitionists felt slavery was wrong. They wrote to newspapers and made pamphlets about the subject, hoping to inform the rest of the population. Over time, slaves began **rebelling** against their masters. Ultimately, these slave rebellions failed, and in an effort to prevent future rebellions, African Americans were punished by being **executed** or whipped.

When Abraham Lincoln became president in 1861, he opposed slavery. People from the southern states became upset and left the **Union**. The Civil War soon started. The North battled the South, with the future of slavery at stake. After the Fourteenth Amendment passed in 1865, and the Union's victory in the Civil War, slavery officially ended.

Abraham Lincoln advocated abolition of slavery, upsetting the Southern states.

Laws and Punishments

Importing slaves from Africa had been a part of the North American culture for many years before the United States became an independent country. Even after independence was achieved, it remained legal to import and own slaves in many states. It was not until January 1, 1808, that importing slaves was made illegal.

Slaves could be bought or even loaned to others. They were passed down from generation to generation in the same family. Children born to slave parents would automatically be considered slaves. Many northern states started granting African Americans citizenship in the early 1800s, but this was put to a stop in 1857. Dred Scott, a slave, believed he had the legal right to freedom because he had, at one time, lived in Illinois and Wisconsin, states where slavery was illegal. He filed a case to the same effect in the state court of Missouri, and after being heard at the state and federal levels, his case reached the **Supreme Court**. The court's historic decision confirmed that slaves were mere property and did not qualify to become citizens. They could be treated in any way their master considered appropriate.

Dred Scott did not sue for his freedom until after his master died in 1843. He moved with his master's widow to Missouri, where slavery was still legal. First, he offered to buy his freedom. When she refused, he took his case to court.

In 1868, the Fourteenth Amendment to the U.S. Constitution was passed. It stated that all people living within the United States had the right to equal protection under the law. This led to all slaves becoming free citizens.

Growing Frustrations

Slave owners exercised control over many aspects of slaves' lives, including education. It was believed that educated slaves were more likely to rebel or encourage other slaves to form a rebellious group. To counter this, laws were made to restrict African Americans from learning to read or write the English language. Anyone caught teaching slaves these skills could be punished for doing so.

African Americans grew frustrated with their situation. They wanted their freedom and began to rebel. The failure of their attempts at freedom made their situation worse. Many African Americans were sent to trial and executed for their actions. In other cases, slave owners committed their own acts of violence against the slaves, even after the slaves stopped rebelling.

New Laws to Prevent Actions

New laws were put in place that made it difficult for slaves to gather and discuss future **revolts**. Those found responsible for planning rebellions would be executed. This caused a great deal of fear among slaves. The fear of being connected to this type of activity caused some African Americans to leak information about pending rebellions to their masters. Some even tried to talk other slaves out of revolting. In a few rare cases, slaves were rewarded for these acts by being granted their freedom.

A Time for Change

Across the United States, people began to take notice of slave rebellions in both the northern and southern states. Primarily in the North, people started demanding the end of slavery. This was further fueled by the talk of abolition among the many slave leaders who believed in freedom for all.

The push for freedom required great leadership, and people began to step forward with ideas about how to end slavery. Many slaves believed that running away from their masters would easily help them find freedom. Other people, such as non-violent abolitionists, promoted the end of slavery and helped slaves leave the South without getting **captured**.

The election of President Abraham Lincoln was one of the factors that led to the Civil War. Lincoln firmly opposed slavery, so Southern states decided to leave the Union, fearing that Lincoln would soon put an end to slavery. This led to the start of the Civil War.

The Civil War and the Emancipation Proclamation

Lincoln realized that, to win the war, he would need the help of African Americans, who were not allowed to fight in the war. On January 1, 1863, the Emancipation Proclamation extended freedom to slaves and an invitation to join the army. This was an important step toward ending slavery. African Americans rushed to join the Union army. The Union won the war in large part due to these new soldiers who, prior to the Emancipation Proclamation, were ineligible to **enlist**.

Abolitionists

Abolitionists were important in the fight to end slavery. They served to inform the public of the conditions slaves faced. Many of the abolitionists were northerners who felt that slavery should not be allowed to continue. They wrote to newspapers and spoke at gatherings to raise awareness.

Some of the best-known abolitionists included Frederick Douglass, who wrote about abolition in his newspaper, *The North Star*, William Lloyd Garrison who wrote in the newspaper *The Liberator*, and Harriet Tubman, who was a conductor of the Underground Railroad.

The New York City Revolt of 1712

The first major slave uprising took place in Manhattan, New York, in 1712. There were almost as many African American slaves living in the southern part of Manhattan as there were colonists of European ancestry. Often, slaves lived near each other. They worked with Africans Americans who had been set free from slavery by their masters in return for money. These free people could move throughout the city and have many friends. Freed slaves could organize gatherings more easily than slaves living in the southern states.

The Act of Aggression

On April 6, 1712, a group of slaves, reacting to terrible treatment from their masters, came together and committed acts of violence. They set fire to a building in central New York City just after midnight. The act caught the colonists by surprise,

In the 1700s, slave markets could be found along the New York harbor.

More than 18 million people live in New York City today. Of these, more than 3.5 million are African Americans.

and they quickly rushed to the area to extinguish the fire. When they arrived, the slaves attacked.

The Response

Armed forces soon arrived on the scene. They captured more than 25 slaves. About 20 were executed as punishment for their actions, and stricter slave laws were put into place. The laws made such an uprising far more difficult to plan in the future. To begin, no more than three slaves were allowed to gather at one time. Slaves could not go out after dark without being accompanied by their masters. If slaves were caught handling firearms, they would be whipped 20 times. Masters were allowed to punish slaves whenever they felt it was necessary, as long as they did not kill or severely injure the slave. Masters who decided to free a slave would be punished with a **fine**, which would be paid to the freed slave. This was ruled in order to discourage masters from freeing any slaves.

Stono Rebellion

On September 9, 1739, chants of "Liberty!" were heard near the Stono River in South Carolina, where about 20 slaves had gathered. The slaves marched south carrying signs printed with the word "Liberty." This march was led by an African American slave named Jemmy Cato. As the group moved along, more slaves joined the march. By the end of the day, nearly 100 slaves had decided to take part.

Some people believe the group started marching after it heard the news that Florida was offering freedom to slaves. Others believe the Security Act of 1739, which required all people of European ancestry to arm themselves on Sundays, may have been a factor in the march. The slaves may have planned to march before the act was passed so that they would not face a threat to their lives.

Responding to the Security Act

The Stono Rebellion took place about three weeks prior to the Security Act becoming law. A group of slaves walked into a store that sold **ammunition** and armed themselves. They killed two shopkeepers working in the store and then started walking

The Stono River is located southwest of Charleston, South Carolina.

south to Wallace's Tavern. The tavern owner was known to be nice to his slaves, so they let him live. The marchers, however, were not so kind to many others that they passed. They chased many people of European ancestry and killed others. Lieutenant Governor Bull managed to get away from these rebels and warned others in the area.

By noon, a group of about 50 slaves had gathered. They killed more than 20 people and marched over 10 miles before the armed forces arrived. Troops killed about 30 slaves, while the others escaped. However, these slaves were soon captured and executed.

After the Stono Rebellion, a new law, known as the Negro Act, was passed in South Carolina in 1740. This law limited the rights of African American slaves. They could no longer gather in groups, grow food for their own use, earn money, or learn how to read. This was done to avoid any future rebellions or acts of violence against masters.

Who Was Cato?

Cato arrived in South Carolina in the 1720s. He came from the central part of Africa, called the Kongo Empire, at a time when Americans were buying slaves to work on rice **plantations**. The Kongo Empire was a Portuguese colony that had adopted Roman Catholic beliefs. The Roman Catholic Church felt slavery was wrong.

Some historians believe that Cato started the march as a way to lead the slaves to Florida, which was controlled by Roman Catholic Spain. Spain treated slaves as humans rather than as property.

Cato was well respected among the slave community. He spoke both Portuguese and English, and used his English skills to forge documents for other slaves. It is not known exactly what happened to Cato after the march, but it is believed that he was among those killed.

1741's Great Plot in New York City

O f the many significant events in the history of slavery, a few that occurred in 1741 are considered crucial in their impact. One such event was the Great Plot, which took place in New York City.

John Hughson was a poor cobbler who had come to New York City in 1730 in search of a better life. After being without work for a long time, he opened a tavern. Most of his clients were African American slaves. On February 28, 1741, two African American slaves broke into a New York shop and stole some valuable silver and coins. The next day, the slaves visited John's tavern. Mary Burton, a 17-year-old servant at the

tavern, learned of the robbery and contacted authorities. She identified the slaves as being responsible for committing the theft, and one slave was arrested. Mary also told the authorities that the tavern owner had received stolen goods from the slaves.

Before authorities could respond to Mary's accusations about John Hughson, a series of fires began across the city and continued through the months of March and April.

What Caused these Actions?
At first, the reasons for the fires were mysterious to all. At the scene of one of the fires, an African American slave was caught stealing. Citizens

and city officials began to think that slaves were trying to burn all of New York City and take over the government. A reward was offered for any information about the conspiracy. **Testimony** came quickly, and many slaves were arrested.

The Results

In May, the two slaves who had committed the February 28 robbery were executed. Two other slaves were set to be hanged, but before they were put to death, they provided a new piece of information. The slaves confessed that John Hughson, the owner of the tavern, had come up with the plan to start the fires and steal. They said that Hughson gave them space in the tavern to hide their stolen goods. The slaves accused many others of being part of the plot as

well. Hughson was arrested, tried, and **convicted**.

Many slaves were questioned about the plan, and fearing for their lives, told authorities what they wanted to hear. Hughson and his wife were hanged. Others believed to be part of the plot were tried throughout the summer. Many were convicted and executed.

About 35 percent of the people who immigrated through the port of New York between 1732 and 1754 were African American slaves.

Gabriel's Fight for Freedom

Born in Virginia in 1776, Gabriel was a big, strong, semi-**literate** African American slave. By his early twenties, many slaves considered Gabriel, a trained blacksmith, a leader. Gabriel worked in Thomas Prosser's tobacco fields. When Thomas Prosser passed away in 1798, his son, Thomas Henry Prosser, took over as the master of the field.

The younger Prosser hired out some of his slaves, including Gabriel, to work elsewhere. During this time, Gabriel was able to make money and socialize with others. He learned their opinions on slavery and the government.

At this time, the **class system** in Virginia was starting to change. Working class people of European ancestry sometimes socialized with free African Americans, as well as slaves. As a result, wealthy people were the minority. Laws were passed to try to prevent the classes from socializing.

Gabriel's Turning Point

In 1799, a man of European ancestry saw Gabriel, his brother Solomon, and another slave stealing a pig. The man tried to stop Gabriel. They fought, and Gabriel bit off most of the man's ear. A trial concluded that Gabriel

Many slaves felt their conditions were unfair and hoped to find equality as U.S. citizens. Gabriel was one such slave.

AM I NOT A MAN & A BROTHER

had **maimed** the man. He was sentenced to a public branding and to spend one month in jail.

By the time he was released from jail, Gabriel had come up with a plan to stand up for the rights of slaves. He wanted to seize bridges and take the Virginia governor, James Monroe, hostage. He would use the bridges and Monroe as leverage to negotiate with the authorities for freedom. Gabriel began organizing slaves to take part in the plan. He believed that poor people from other cultures would also join the fight.

The plan was to take place on August 30, 1800, but heavy rains forced Gabriel to **postpone** his plan. Before he had a chance to move into action, two slaves informed their masters of the plan. The masters warned the governor, who called for the **militia**. Gabriel and others tried to escape to Norfolk, Virginia, but they were captured and later executed.

Slaves worked hard at daily tasks. They did household chores and worked the land.

Louisiana Slave Revolt of 1811

January 9, 1811, was the date of one of the largest slave revolts in United States history. A group of slaves, led by Charles Deslondes, attacked the owner of the Manuel Andry sugar plantation. The group believed that the plantation, located just outside of New Orleans, housed a huge collection of weapons. However, they found that the weapons were not there. Upset with their findings, they killed the plantation owner's son.

During revolts, slaves often tried to escape capture, but few were successful.

Already armed with an assortment of weapons, including a few guns, clubs, tools, and cane knives, the slaves decided to follow through with a planned march to New Orleans. Most slaves they encountered along the way joined the march. Deslondes expected that, by the time the group reached New Orleans, it would be large enough to overwhelm authorities. He thought the slaves would be able to take over New Orleans and turn it into a free land for all southern slaves.

Deslondes' Poor Judgment

The slaves reached New Orleans as planned. However, news about their killings had already spread through the sugar plantations. There, people of European ancestry raised their own militia and received assistance from the U.S. troops stationed in Baton Rouge. Under the leadership of Major Charles Perret, the local Fifth Militia Regiment was ready to fight back. When they attacked the slave group, the troops discovered that they were grossly outnumbered, and the Fifth Militia quickly **retreated**.

The next day, federal troops arrived on the scene to help the militia. Deslondes and several others managed to escape. Many of the slaves were killed or were forced to surrender.

However, many of the escaped slaves, including Deslondes, were captured from the farm where they had set up their camp and later faced trial. Seven were granted freedom when they proved that they had tried to stop the revolt from occurring. About 30 slaves claimed they had been forced to join the battle. They were returned to their owners. However, Deslondes and 20 others were found guilty and executed.

SLAVERY QUICK FACTS

At the time of the Louisiana revolt, Charles Deslondes was a free African American man in his thirties who worked as a farm laborer near New Orleans.

The local Fifth Militia Regiment sent about 20 men to the farm where Deslondes and the slaves had set up their camp.

Fifty slaves were returned to their masters despite stating that they had not been forced to join the march.

New Orleans was a major slave trade port.

George Boxley's Rebellion of 1815

Slavery was viewed as a great injustice by African American slaves, as well as many people of other cultural backgrounds and social classes. George Boxley was one of those people.

Boxley was a storekeeper and farmer of European ancestry who lived in Spotsylvania County, Virginia. He felt that the inequalities between rich and poor were far too great. Boxley thought that this was reflected in the government, which was dominated by wealthy supporters of slavery.

In an effort to change this, Boxley unsuccessfully ran for a position in the state legislature. Still, by 1815, Boxley decided to take a stand against slavery.

Boxley's plan was to attack and take over Fredericksburg and Richmond, Virginia, and free the slaves there. Slaves from the area took an active role in planning the uprising, and they helped collect weapons.

A Slave Second-guesses the Plan
One of the slaves, Lucy, was not entirely convinced that it was a good

idea to take part in the rebellion. She told the plan to her master, Ptolemy Powell, who informed authorities. Many of the slaves were arrested, and later, some were executed.

Boxley was arrested and jailed. With the use of a file that his wife gave him during a visit, Boxley cut his chains and escaped from jail. Rewards were offered for Boxley's capture, but he was never found. Various accounts by historians indicate that he and his family escaped to Indiana.

The Underground Railroad

In the early 1800s, the Underground Railroad was responsible for helping about 100,000 slaves gain their freedom. The system was not actually a railway, but rather a series of safe houses and secret routes that were used to help slaves escape. Abolitionists and free African Americans acted as "conductors" on the Underground Railroad. They were responsible for helping slaves get to free states in the North and, sometimes, Canada.

In most cases, slaves had to find a way to escape from their owners. Sometimes, conductors would enter plantations pretending to be slaves. Once inside, the conductors would help slaves escape. After their escape, slaves would begin the long trip north. They traveled along secret routes by train, boat, or on foot, stopping at safe houses along the way. At each stop, slaves would receive help from free people who gave them a place to rest, food to eat, and money for the rest of their trip.

Once a slave left a safe house, a message was sent to alert the next stop that the slave was on his or her way. When slaves arrived in their new northern home, they received help finding a place to work.

Denmark Vesey's Uprising of 1822

An important event in the history of slavery was the uprising of 1822 in Charleston, South Carolina. Denmark Vesey was a West Indian slave who had won a lottery with a big cash prize. He paid for his freedom with his winnings and ended his own slavery. However, he never forgot his life as a slave and wanted to help free other slaves who were subjected to poor treatment at the hands of their masters. As a result, Vesey planned the fincr details of a revolt that was to take place in July 1822.

Planning an Uprising

Vesey studied the Bible. He used quotes from it to help prove to slaves that slavery was a sin that they must fight. This helped him get the support he needed to launch the revolt.

Vesey shared many of his ideas at an African church where he was well respected. African priest Gullah Jack Pritchard was one of Vesey's top supporters. With Gullah Jack Pritchard, Vesey gained the trust of the congregation. He organized African American slaves and prepared them for their roles in their fight for freedom. Vesey told the slaves that they would be helped by the people of Santo Domingo, as well as Africa, if the slaves made the first move. Vesey's plan called for the slaves to murder their masters and take control of Charleston, South Carolina.

Vesey's efforts to spread his ideas worked, and thousands of slaves heard about his plan through the church or by word of mouth. Most of them agreed, but because word had spread so far, his plan was revealed before it could be launched. Hundreds of slaves reported the details to their masters or were overheard discussing them with others. If the plan had been put in place, it had the potential to have a huge impact on the lives of slaves.

When the news spread, Charleston authorities went into action and caught those responsible for planning the revolt. These people were **deported** or executed. Vesey was among the more than 30 people executed for their efforts in planning the revolt. African American slaves who watched the executions wore black clothes. This was seen as an act of mourning and disobedience.

The Haitian Revolution

Prior to Denmark Vesey's planning of the 1822 uprising, another event had captured his attention. The Haitian Revolution took place between 1791 and 1804. It is believed to be the most successful slave rebellion to have ever taken place in the western world.

Vesey talked to slaves about the details of the Haitian Revolution. He told them that, when the revolution began, Haiti was a colony of France called Saint Dominigue. Under the leadership of a former slave named Toussaint L'Ouverture, the slaves defeated British forces. Then, L'Ouverture began running the land as an independent state instead of surrendering control back to the country of France. L'Ouverture was captured, but eventually, France was defeated, and the new independent country of Haiti was born.

Whenever Vesey recruited slaves, he always used the Haitian Revolution as an example of how to defeat masters. The story had an effect on the slaves, and they wanted to repeat this kind of success themselves.

Nat Turner's Rebellion of 1831

Nat Turner was born on October 2, 1800, as a slave of Benjamin Turner. When Benjamin Turner died, Nat became the slave of other members of the Turner family. Nat was sold in 1823 to Thomas Moore. When Thomas Moore passed away, Nat was passed down to Moore's son, Putnam. Putnam was young, so his mother's new husband, Joseph Travis, became Nat's master. Nat considered Joseph Travis a very kind master and never had any problems with him. However, Nat firmly believed that slavery was wrong and must be **abolished**.

A Sign from God?

Nat noticed a **solar eclipse** in February 1831 and considered it a sign from God to take action against slavery. He told his four closest slave friends his plans, and, together, they decided to stage a revolt on July 4. By the time July 4 came, Nat was ill, and the revolt was postponed. Nat believed God would give him a sign to begin his revolt on a different day. On August 13, when the Sun appeared bluish-green in color due to atmospheric conditions, Nat took this as the sign that the time had come for the slaves to rebel.

Nat met with six slaves on August 21 to plan the revolt. He did not let many slaves know about the plan. Nat had learned from experience that, sometimes, plans were leaked to masters, and he did not want the revolt to be stopped before it had started. After the small group discussed the plan, they immediately went into action.

The Slaves begin their Rebellion

The slaves began putting their plans in action at the Travis household. Even though he thought highly of his master, Nat killed the entire Travis family as

Nat Turner was captured and later executed.

they slept. This act was indicative of the type of rebellion Nat planned to lead. Throughout the rebellion, Nat treated all people of European ancestry equally, regardless of age or gender. He showed no kindness for women or children. Nat planned to kill any people of European ancestry he could find. The group continued from home to home killing any people of European ancestry they encountered.

Along the way, more slaves joined Nat's group. At each house, they killed the people inside and collected weapons. By the end of the first full day, the group had grown to more than 50 slaves. They marched on toward Jerusalem, Virginia. People of European ancestry had begun to take notice of the group and prepared for battle. They confronted the slaves, killing a few of them. Some of the slaves decided to retreat. Nat and many others continued to press forward. All of Nat's remaining supporters were captured or killed by August 24. Nat was left alone on his journey.

Nat went into hiding. Militia in the area went on a rampage, punishing African Americans for these acts. Nat successfully hid for more than two months. On October 30, he was found and was put on trial. He received a guilty sentence on November 5, and on November 11, he was executed.

SLAVERY QUICK FACTS

Within a day of the revolt's outbreak, Nat increased the size of his group to 50 people strong.

While hiding from authorities, Nat Turner spent most of his time near the Travis farm.

The state of Maryland responded to Nat Turner's Rebellion by banning any free African Americans from other areas to enter into its state.

Virginia Reconsiders Slavery

The events of Nat Turner's Rebellion caused many in Virginia to reconsider slavery. They began to wonder if the low cost of slave labor was worth the dangers of potential rebellions. Many refused to consider the idea that African Americans were rebelling because they were not being treated fairly and wanted to be free. Slave owners were convinced that slavery was a tradition and a positive part of society.

There was growing support for abolishing slavery. A **committee** reviewed the idea but decided against it. Instead, new laws were put into place. Virginian African Americans were no longer allowed to sell or purchase liquor, learn to read or write, or to preach. Other states reacted to Nat Turner's Rebellion by creating laws they felt would prevent a similar event.

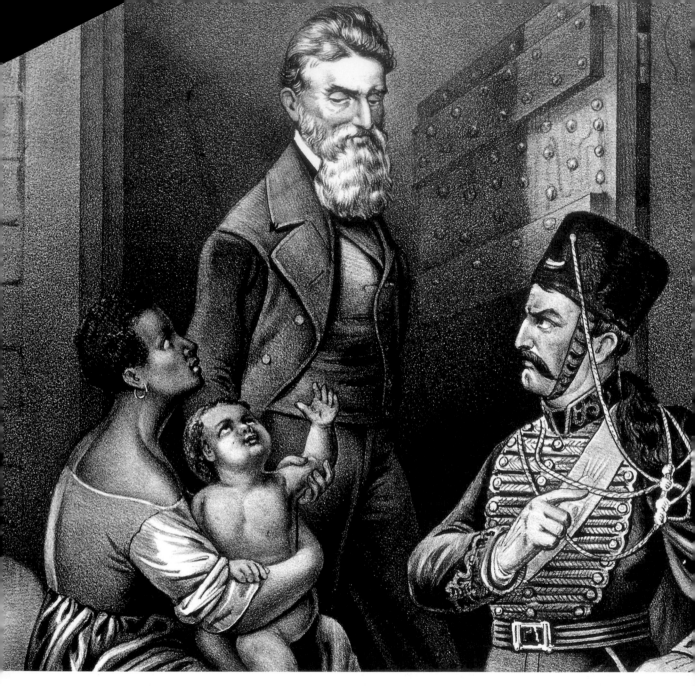

Factors Behind the Revolts

With one uprising after another hitting the country, most people felt that the abolitionist movement was one of the biggest reasons the revolts were happening. The revolts were summed up as the consequences of abolitionist leaders talking to various slaves and educating them about their right to freedom. Some abolitionists, such as John Brown, were people of European ancestry who were doing

William Lloyd Garrison faced many anti-abolitionist lynch mobs for his beliefs about the abolition of slavery.

whatever they could to help African American slaves stand up to their masters. Abolitionists wrote about their ideas and tried to spread their vision of a world without slavery. David Walker and William Lloyd Garrison were two of the most popular abolitionist writers of the day. They used the written word to share their ideas about freedom and the end of slavery. Their words inspired slaves to take a stand against the power of their masters. Slaves who could read, read Walker's and Garrison's articles aloud to others. This created a pool of slaves ready to take on their masters.

David Walker

David Walker was born a free African American in North Carolina in 1785. He wrote the anti-slavery pamphlet *Walker's Appeal*, which called for "black pride" amongst slaves. Walker advocated violent rebellion as a way to achieve freedom. The pamphlet helped shape debates about limits on free speech more than three decades before the Civil War and the subsequent ratification of the Fourteenth Amendment.

William Lloyd Garrison

William Lloyd Garrison and other abolitionists began getting the attention of slaves and their masters. To slaves, abolitionists were like friends who would help them directly when given the opportunity. Abolitionists put the spotlight on all of the injustices involved with slavery. This made the abolitionists enemies of the masters.

Early Beginnings

William Lloyd Garrison was born in Newburyport, Massachusetts in 1805. His father left the family when Garrison was very young.

The family was poor, and Garrison was forced to work as a young boy so he could buy food and other necessary things to survive.

Garrison was a bright, hardworking boy. As a teenager, he took a job as a writer and editor for the *Newburyport Herald*. At the age of 25, Garrison joined the abolitionist movement. He moved to Baltimore, Maryland, to work for the anti-slavery newspaper, *Genius of Universal Emancipation*. While with the newspaper, he wrote about the immediate need for the end of slavery.

William Lloyd Garrison, American abolitionist, printer, and journalist, published *The Liberator* in Boston, Massachusetts. He used the paper to advocate the abolition of slavery in the South.

Arguing for Freedom

Garrison's columns and speeches were met with a great deal of criticism. Many who read his columns believed he was an African American man. They were surprised when they learned he was of European ancestry and began attacking his ideas. Slavery supporters argued that, even if African Americans were freed, they would not be able to adapt to society. Garrison believed that, if slaves were given a fair opportunity and time to transition, they would be equally productive members of society.

Inspiring Change

In 1831, Garrison started his own anti-slavery newspaper called *The Liberator*. At first, there were few subscriptions to the newspaper. However, Garrison continued to provide the latest news of abuse, kidnappings, and murders committed against slaves. Over time, the abolitionist movement and subscriptions to his newspaper grew. People became more informed and interested in seeing slavery end. The final issue of the newspaper came out in 1865, at the end of the Civil War and the abolition of slavery.

Good Friends or Bitter Enemies?

One of the many people William Lloyd Garrison inspired was Frederick Douglass. Douglass was a slave in Maryland. When he escaped from slavery and moved to the northern United States, Douglass began reading Garrison's columns and attended a speech given by Garrison. Garrison later became a fan of Douglass.

Although both men were anti-slavery leaders, they had different opinions about slavery. They disagreed about the position of the United States Constitution in regard to slavery. Garrison felt that the Constitution was pro-slavery and was seen burning copies of it. Douglass felt that the United States Constitution was an important document in the fight against slavery. This led to a major rift between these two leading abolitionists. Douglass' anti-slavery newspaper, *The North Star*, created even more tension. Garrison viewed Douglass' newspaper as inferior competition. Their feud lasted for about 20 years.

Amistad:
Revolt on the Ocean

In July 1839, about 50 Africans successfully revolted aboard a Spanish ship named the *Amistad*. They had been taken violently from their families in West Africa and were sent to Cuba, where they were forced to become slaves.

The Ship Sails

Pedro Montes and Jose Ruiz had purchased slaves at an auction in Havana, Cuba. Spain had banned its territories from bringing in new slaves, but the two slave owners secured the right to move the slaves from one Cuban port to another.

The slaves, Ruiz, Montes, the ship captain, a crewmember, and a cook set sail for Puerto Principe, Cuba. On July 2, under the leadership of an African named Joseph Cinque, the Africans broke free from their shackles and rebelled. They killed the cook and the ship's captain. Two slaves were killed in the revolt. The slaves demanded they be returned home to Africa. Ruiz and Montes agreed, but they had other plans.

During the day, Ruiz and Montes steered the ship east to satisfy the Africans' demands. At night, they steered the ship north, hoping they would be spotted by the British slave patrol and saved from the Africans.

The trip should only have lasted about three days, and instead, the

ship sailed for two months. Conditions onboard worsened daily. Food was rationed, and eight more Africans died.

Taking into consideration the hunger and thirst of his fellow Africans, Cinque finally allowed Montes to approach land. Once docked at Long Island, Cinque and several others left the ship to buy food.

Stories of the slaves and their revolt spread throughout Long Island, and soon the U.S. Navy had put out word for the capture of the ship. Lieutenant Thomas Gedney, commander of the USS *Washington*, boarded the *Amistad*. He questioned Cinque, Montes, and Ruiz. After their discussions, the Africans, ship, and **cargo** were seized on August 27, 1839, and sent to Connecticut.

Joseph Cinque led the rebellion on the *Amistad*. Joseph and his army of slaves killed the cook and the captain and demanded to be sent back home.

Trials and Tribulations

United States Federal District Justice Andrew T. Judson referred the case to Connecticut and the U.S. Circuit Court. The Africans were sent to a New Haven jail while they waited for the court proceedings in Hartford, Connecticut. They were charged as murderers, and their status of being free individuals or slaves was uncertain. Ruiz and Montes continued to argue that the Africans should be returned to Cuba to serve as slaves.

Abolitionists Speak Up

Soon, the story reached local newspapers. New York abolitionists united to help the Africans. They hoped that this case may end slavery. Funds were raised for the Africans' defense. **Interpreters** were found so the Africans could communicate with their lawyer, Roger Sherman Baldwin.

Captain Ferrer was killed in the fight that broke out on the *Amistad* in July 1839.

Roger Sherman Baldwin, the lawyer representing the slaves from the *Amistad*, argued that, because African slave trade was illegal in the Spanish Empire, the Africans were free men. The U.S. and Spanish governments argued that the slaves were not free because they were born before slavery became illegal.

The trial gained attention across the country. Cinque gave his testimony detailing the entire experience aboard the fateful *Amistad*. Justice Judson ruled that the Africans were to be returned to Africa. The U.S. district attorney immediately appealed. Abolitionists viewed it as the first step toward ending slavery.

South Carolina Senator John C. Calhoun, later an advocate of state rights, introduced the idea that any ship seized would come under the authority of the ship's home country. The idea soon was passed as law.

In April 1840, New Haven's Circuit Court referred the appeal to the U.S. Supreme Court. Massachusetts **congressman** and former president of the United States John Quincy Adams stepped in on the side of the Africans and brought the issue to the **House of Representatives**.

Roger Sherman Baldwin, who represented the slaves from *Amistad*, was firm on his stance that slavery was illegal and the slaves should be judged on the current laws.

Senator John C. Calhoun was responsible for the passing of the law that any ship seized would come under the authority of its home country and not the country to which it was traveling.

The Supreme Court case began on February 22, 1841. The Supreme Court affirmed the status of the Africans as free men who could return to Africa. It was further declared that the Africans were not murderers but kidnapping victims.

Africans Tour the United States

After the trial, the Africans were taught English. They began telling their story at public appearances. These appearances had been set up by the abolitionists to help the Africans make money so they could return to Africa. By 1842, the Africans had returned home to Western Africa.

At the time that he was kidnapped in Africa, Cinque was married with children.

After serving as vice president under John Quincy Adams and Andrew Jackson, John C. Calhoun went on to become a leading advocate of state rights.

Roger Sherman Baldwin became the Governor of Connecticut in 1847.

In 1997, Steven Spielberg directed a movie called *Amistad*. The movie details the events on the ship.

Frederick Douglass

Frederick Douglass was born a Maryland slave in February 1818. His mother was a slave, and he never met his father.

Douglass was raised by his grandparents and one of his aunts. He saw his mother only a few times before she died when he was about seven. At the age of eight, Douglass was sent to live with a shipbuilder in Baltimore, Maryland. He was taught to read and write, and he learned about the abolitionist movement. Douglass read newspapers and political pamphlets, which exposed him to the meaning of human rights and freedom.

The Last Straw

In 1833, Douglass' master sent him to work on a farm for Edward Covey. Covey was well known for being rough with slaves, and he beat Douglass regularly. Douglass became desperate to gain his freedom. He made a promise to himself to escape and become a free man.

Douglass' first two attempts to escape failed, and he spent some time in jail. However, on September 3, 1838, Douglass boarded a train and successfully escaped. By the next day, he had arrived in New York. A few weeks later, Douglass moved to New Bedford, Massachusetts.

The New Free Life

With his new free life, Douglass was able to join groups, including an African American church and abolitionist organizations. He subscribed to William Lloyd Garrison's newspaper, *The Liberator*. He found Garrison's views informative

From a young age, Frederick Douglass was keen on getting an education.

and inspiring. Douglass spoke at the Anti-Slavery Society's Nantucket convention. He was asked to return as a featured lecturer.

Communicating with the People

This paved the way for Douglass' future. Douglass spoke to people about slavery. He wrote an autobiography, *Narrative of the Life of Frederick Douglass, an American Slave*, which was published in 1845. He further promoted anti-slavery with his newspaper, *The North Star*.

Douglass also stressed the importance of education for African American slaves. He wanted to create awareness about their right to freedom and better opportunities.

During the Civil War, Douglass spoke with President Abraham Lincoln and helped sign up northern African Americans to serve in the Union Army. His influence on the United States extended far after slavery ended. He continued to demand equality for all humans and remained a powerful political figure for the rest of his life.

Harriet Tubman

Harriet Tubman helped many slaves through her work on the Underground Railroad. Tubman was born Araminta Ross in Dorchester County, Maryland, around 1820.

Ross began working as a slave at about five or six years of age. As a teenager, a slave owner demanded her help when one of his slaves tried to escape. Ross refused.

In her mid-twenties, Ross married a free African American man named John Tubman and changed her name to Harriet Tubman. In 1849, she escaped from slavery and moved to Philadelphia, Pennsylvania. Soon after, Tubman returned to Maryland to help her sister and her children escape. With that success, she decided to help other slaves.

The **Fugitive** Slave Act of 1850 stated that slaves who escaped to free land were still slaves and were required to return to their masters. To get around this law, Tubman sent escaped slaves into Canada. Here, they would not be returned to a life of slavery. She became a wanted woman in the South. Big rewards were offered for her capture. Still, Tubman continued to help hundreds of slaves find their freedom.

Emancipation

The 1860 presidential election played a crucial role in the fight to end slavery. Prior to the election, Republican nominee Abraham Lincoln made it clear to voters that he opposed slavery. When Lincoln won the election, Southerners were very upset. They felt as though they no longer wanted to be part of the United States.

On December 20, 1860, less than eight weeks after the election, the state of South Carolina decided to separate from the rest of the nation.

Soon, more states decided to follow. Mississippi, Florida, Alabama, Georgia, Louisiana, and Texas had all left the Union by the beginning of February 1861.

The Civil War Begins

The seven states that had left the Union combined to create the **Confederate** States of America. Jefferson Davis was named the provisional president of the Confederacy. In Lincoln's inaugural address on March 4, 1861, he stated that he hoped to reunite the country. The Confederate states offered to pay for the federal properties within their borders, but Lincoln refused to negotiate. On April 12, 1861, the Confederate States attacked Fort Sumter in Charleston, South Carolina, to make the Union surrender the property. Fort Sumter was the most important piece of government property held by the Union. When the federal troops fought back, the Civil War officially began.

Tennessee, Arkansas, North Carolina, and Virginia immediately joined the Confederacy after the attack. President Lincoln responded by stating that the Civil War was about bringing the Union back together and not about ending slavery. The states had originally separated over the slavery issue. Lincoln knew that Northerners supported the end of slavery, but they did not want to fight a war to make this happen.

African Americans volunteered to join the northern army, but they were rejected, as existing laws prevented their participation. This helped to reinforce Lincoln's statements about the role slavery played in the war.

As the war progressed, the northern army met with many African American fugitives from the South. The Union did its best to provide for them, but it was difficult. Many fugitives were packed into small camps. The conditions were far from ideal, and many died from starvation and disease. Concerned Northerners offered to help in any way they could.

The Emancipation Proclamation

Although African Americans in the North were not able to help fight against the Confederates, slaves in the Confederate States were forced to help their masters fight against the Union.

The second Battle of Fort Wagner, on July 18, 1863, was led by one of the first major U.S. military units made up of African American troops.

African Americans in Richmond, Virginia, crowded around President Lincoln after Richmond was captured by Union troops.

In September 1862, the Union won the Battle of Antietam, and Lincoln announced the freeing of slaves. Lincoln stated that, if the Confederate States did not surrender by January 1, 1863, their slaves would be legally free citizens. This became known as the Emancipation Proclamation.

The deadline passed, and the Civil War officially shifted from being about preserving the Union to bringing about the end of slavery. All of the slaves in the Confederate States were considered free citizens. Most, however, did not find out about the proclamation until many months had passed. African Americans in the North celebrated and were allowed to join the army. Many quickly volunteered.

While they were allowed to join the army, African Americans still faced **discrimination**. Their pay and supplies were noticeably inferior to soldiers of European ancestry. Some soldiers refused to fight alongside African Americans.

Confederate slaves joined the Union as soon as Northern troops entered their area. The Confederates lost many slaves during the battle, and other issues created problems. Wealthy

Southerners were not required to fight the war. This angered most of the working-class people who believed they were fighting a war that would eventually only benefit the rich. This made it difficult for the Confederacy to continue to fight.

The War Ends

The Confederacy surrendered on April 18, 1865. In the end, more than 600,000 people died in the fight, while thousands more were injured. The **Thirteenth Amendment** was passed, abolishing slavery and proclaiming the Union victor in the Civil War.

Reconstruction

Following the Civil War, four million African Americans had their first taste of freedom. Many African Americans used this freedom to travel around the country. They visited family and friends. For the first time, they had the freedom to do almost everything that people of European ancestry could do.

This time in history became known as the **Reconstruction** period. It was a time to rebuild the country. In particular, the southern United States was in poor condition. Without slaves, masters wondered how they would rebuild their plantations. Meanwhile, African Americans had new responsibilities, such as finding jobs and places to live.

Reconstruction was a difficult process for everyone as African Americans learned to adjust to new ways of living. The era lasted until 1877.

Struggling for Equality

Following the end of the Civil War, African Americans faced many new opportunities. They had to find places to live and jobs so that they could make money. As slaves, they had developed valuable skills working, but they did not have to search for work. For the first time, African Americans found themselves competing in the job market against each other, as well as against people of other cultures.

In February 1869, the Fifteenth Amendment was passed. This guaranteed all African Americans the right to vote.

Discrimination Persists

Even after achieving freedom from slavery, African Americans still faced discrimination and segregation. Many people of European ancestry did not view African Americans as equal members of society. African Americans were kept from attaining true equality by an imposed class

Malcolm X, a civil rights leader, firmly believed that African Americans should fight for their rights using any means necessary.

structure. While some African Americans were able to attend school, others were not. Many were also refused services in stores. Though they were no longer slaves, African Americans still had to fight for their equality and **civil rights**.

Civil Rights Movement

With the turn of the century, new leaders emerged in the fight for civil rights. Some of these people took a peaceful approach. Martin Luther King, Jr., a minister in the mid-1900s, used inspiring words to help people across the nation understand why African Americans should be granted their civil rights. Others, such as Malcolm X, an African American Muslim minister and the spokesperson of the Nation of Islam around the 1940s, declared that African Americans should earn their civil rights by any means necessary.

After King was assassinated in 1968, his words continued to inspire. Soon, African Americans were met with greater opportunities. Today, most African Americans are given the same opportunities as other U.S. citizens.

Timeline

1619: Africans are captured and brought to Jamestown, Virginia, to work as slaves.

1619

1807: Congress declares it illegal to bring slaves into the United States.

1831-1861: About 75,000 slaves escape by the Underground Railroad, a network that helped protect and hide escaped slaves so they could find freedom.

1861: The Civil War begins. One of the main issues behind the conflict is to determine if slavery should be allowed.

1863: President Abraham Lincoln passes the Emancipation Proclamation, which legally frees all slaves.

1865: Congress passes the Thirteenth Amendment, which outlaws slavery.

1866: Congress passes the Civil Rights Act, which declares African Americans as citizens.

1881: The first Jim Crow Law is passed in Tennessee.

1896: In *Plessy v. Ferguson*, the Supreme Court rules that public places may be segregated as long as equal facilities are given to African Americans.

1909: The National Association for the Advancement of Colored People (NAACP) is formed.

1909

1910-1920: During a period known as the Great Migration, about 500,000 African Americans move to northern states.

1861

1914: Marcus Garvey forms the Universal Negro Improvement Association in Jamaica. The group eventually opens branches in the United States.

1919: A series of violent events occur in response to the Great Migration. The period is known as "Red Summer" because of the hundreds of deaths that resulted from the violence.

1942: The Congress of Racial Equality (CORE) is started in Chicago.

1948: President Truman desegregates the army.

1954: In *Brown v. Board of Education of Topeka*, the Supreme Court rules against school segregation.

1955: The Montgomery Bus Boycott begins when Rosa Parks refuses to give up her seat to a passenger of European ancestry.

1957: A community in Little Rock, Arkansas opposes desegregation and plans a protest to prevent nine African American students from entering a school that was formerly for students of European ancestry. The African American students are later called the "Little Rock Nine."

1960: At a Woolworth's lunch counter in Greensboro, North Carolina, four African American college students hold the first sit-in.

1961: The Congress of Racial Equality (CORE) begins to organize Freedom Rides.

1963

1963: Martin Luther King, Jr. writes "Letter from a Birmingham Jail."

1964: Martin Luther King, Jr. is awarded the Nobel Peace Prize.

1965: Malcolm X is assassinated in New York.

1961

1983: Astronaut Guion "Guy" S. Bluford, Jr., becomes the first African American in space, flying aboard the space shuttle *Challenger*.

1985: Philadelphia State Police bomb a house in Philadelphia occupied by an African American activist organization, MOVE, killing 11 occupants and triggering a fire that destroyed a neighborhood and left more than 300 people homeless.

1986: Martin Luther King, Jr.'s birthday is made into a national holiday.

1989: General Colin L. Powell is the first African American to be named chair of the Joint Chiefs of Staff of the U.S. military.

1989: Oprah Winfrey becomes the first African American woman to host a nationally syndicated talk show.

2008

2008: Barack Obama, a politician from Chicago's South Side, becomes the first African American to be elected president of the United States.

2012: President Obama is elected for a second term.

Activity

Making a Difference

What does it take to make a difference in politics? Politicians are the people who guide changes in society, but they need input from the people they represent. They need to hear a variety of opinions before they act. In this activity, you will develop an idea that you would like to see become a law.

First, think about things that affect your life. Is there a social issue that concerns you? Can you think of a new law that can affect this issue? Research on the internet to learn about this issue. Try to find different opinions about the issue.

Now, think about some of the ways you can peacefully affect political change. Write down your ideas on a piece of paper. Then, create a plan to put these thoughts into effect. You should make sure that your ideas are well researched and offer valid solutions. Ideas that are not valid will weaken your plan.

Finally, write a letter outlining your ideas to a political leader. Introduce the issue in your opening paragraph. In the next paragraphs, present your ideas to bring about change. Conclude your letter with a summary of all of the important points you mentioned in the introductory paragraph.

You will need:

✓ a pen
✓ paper
✓ access to the internet

Test Your Knowledge

1 In what South Carolina city did Denmark Vesey attempt his rebellion?

Charleston

2 Who was the leader of the Stono Rebellion?

Cato

3 When Harriet Tubman escaped, where did she relocate?

Philadelphia, Pennsylvania

4 Which state was the first to leave the United States of America?

South Carolina

5 When did William Lloyd Garrison first publish the anti-slavery newspaper, *The Liberator*?

1831

6 What was the new requirement in the 1739 Security Act?

All people of European ancestry had to arm themselves on Sundays.

Key Words

abolished: put an end to something

abolitionists: people working to ensure that slavery ends

ammunition: something that is fired from a gun

armed forces: a country's military

captured: when a person or object is forcibly controlled

cargo: goods found in a large moving vehicle

civil rights: basic rights that are guaranteed to citizens of a country

class system: when people are grouped according to something they have in common

committee: an impartial group responsible for reviews

Confederate: the states that combined to oppose the Union

congressman: an individual in the House of Representatives

convicted: found guilty of a crime

deported: sent out of a country

discrimination: unfair treatment due to prejudice

enlist: join the military

executed: put to death

fine: a penalty where the guilty party has to pay a certain amount of money

fugitive: a person who is being hunted by others

House of Representatives: along with the Senate, it is one of two chambers in the United States Congress

interpreters: people who translate languages

literate: able to read and write

maimed: to be disabled or disfigured, usually by depriving of the use of a limb or other part of the body

masters: people in charge of slaves

militia: people who are trained as soldiers but are not a part of an actual army

plantations: large farms that produce crops, including tobacco, cotton, and sugar

postpone: put off until a later date

pounds sterling: the currency of Great Britain

rebelling: organizing uprisings in which a group tries to take power from authority figures

Reconstruction: the period between 1865 and 1877 in which southern states tried to rebuild and adapt to the new ways of living in the United States

retreated: withdrew and went to a safer position or place

revolts: uprisings against authority

solar eclipse: a time when the Moon passes in front of the Sun, sometimes creating a temporary blackout

Supreme Court: the highest court of the United States

testimony: a statement given under oath

Thirteenth Amendment: an official change to the U.S. Constitution that made slavery illegal

Union: the original U.S. states that remained together during the Civil War

Index

Log on to www.av2books.com

AV² by Weigl brings you media enhanced books that support active learning. Go to www.av2books.com, and enter the special code found on page 2 of this book. You will gain access to enriched and enhanced content that supplements and complements this book. Content includes video, audio, weblinks, quizzes, a slide show, and activities.

AV² Online Navigation

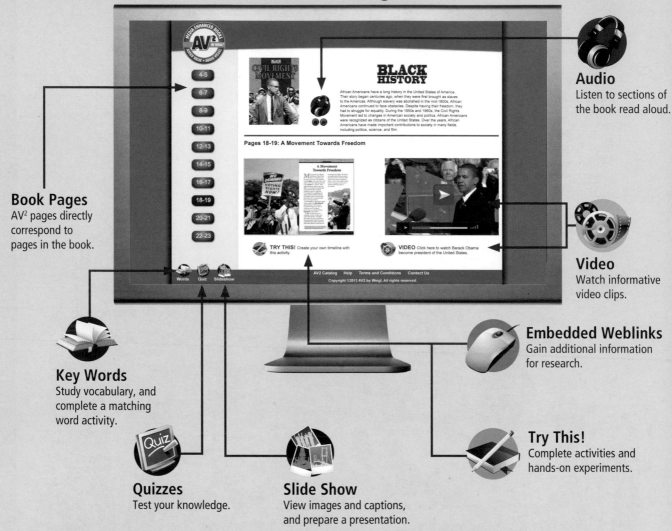

Audio
Listen to sections of the book read aloud.

Book Pages
AV² pages directly correspond to pages in the book.

Video
Watch informative video clips.

Key Words
Study vocabulary, and complete a matching word activity.

Embedded Weblinks
Gain additional information for research.

Quizzes
Test your knowledge.

Slide Show
View images and captions, and prepare a presentation.

Try This!
Complete activities and hands-on experiments.

AV² was built to bridge the gap between print and digital. We encourage you to tell us what you like and what you want to see in the future.

Sign up to be an AV² Ambassador at www.av2books.com/ambassador.

Due to the dynamic nature of the Internet, some of the URLs and activities provided as part of AV² by Weigl may have changed or ceased to exist. AV² by Weigl accepts no responsibility for any such changes. All media enhanced books are regularly monitored to update addresses and sites in a timely manner. Contact AV² by Weigl at 1-866-649-3445 or av2books@weigl.com with any questions, comments, or feedback.